Writing Place

A Collection of Writings
From
Lapidus Scotland's
'Writing Place and Space'

Edited by
Margot Henderson

Front Cover photo by Caren Gilbert
Back Cover by Philippa Johnston
Cover design by Stewart Forbes

Other Photos by

St Andrews by Jayne Wilding
Moniack Mhor courtesy of Moniack
Lochinver by Philippa Johnston
Falkland courtesy of Falkland Centre for Stewardship
Abriachan by Christine Mathieson
Glasgow Tenement Painting by Andy Xaoi
Dysart by Caren Gilbert.

Foreword

What on earth was I thinking of when I took this on! Can you imagine trying to put this anthology together! Having to make choices in selecting work that would give a true representation of a whole year's worth of writing by over 300 writers in response to such diverse locations. Well after much contemplation, appreciation and agonising...this is it! Please bear in mind that this is only a fraction of the writing actually done, not all writers chose to submit work, other writers sent a lot.

In selecting pieces, I have set the writing in chronological order, following the cycle of workshops through the year.
I hope this will help to give a feel for the various locations and some sense of the writing journey we took once we got there.

I have placed the writings within the context of the workshops and sequenced them to reflect the flow of the workshop to give a sense of how one activity followed another, showing the movement from inner reflection, to outer exploration.

I have tried to represent the range of prompts, the individual approach of the tutors, the particular style of the writers, and the felt sense of each place.

These writings show how much we are touched by place, in so many ways, how much we need that sense of space to contemplate. It is often when we are in nature that we come closer to our own nature, seeing how place can be a metaphor, a mirror of the self, where the inner and outer landscapes merge.

I hope you enjoy the writings and that you will take some space for yourself to try out some of these writing prompts from place to place.

Margot Henderson
Editor

Contents

Anam Cara

St Andrews

Moniack Mhor

Lochinver

Not Your Time   Lesley O' Brien

Dysart

Dysart Haibun   Jayne Wilding
Exploration of Sense
Small Acts of Rebellion   Caren Gilbert

Downhill in Dysart
Blinded by sight   Elspeth Salter

Untitled   Craig Gilbert

An Appropriate Scale
Sign of the Times   Elspeth Salter

**Abriachan Forest
(Branching Out)**

Forest Haiku   Margot
This Moment   Nathalie,
                                                        Bethany
Branching Out   Bethany, Nathalie
                                                        and Callum
Tree Song   Anne Marie
This Forest Is   Kevin, Grace, David,
                                                        Group, Dominic
My Cathedral   .   Christine

Glenurquhart Elders Group

Here In The Forest
Trees   Amanda, Avis, Eileen
                                                        Elizabeth, Jackie, Jessie

The Places We Love Best   Jim, John, John and
                                                        Margaret

Introduction

'Writing Place, Space and Landscape for Wellbeing' was a year-long LAPIDUS Scotland project which took place during 2014. The aim was to explore how creative writing, reading and storytelling can help us to understand the ways in which place affects our wellbeing.

From November 2013 to October 2014, we delivered a total of 23 writing events in coastal, rural and urban settings across the Highlands, Fife, Glasgow and Edinburgh, attracting over 300 people. These sessions were aimed at three target groups: people with mental health problems, the wider public, and professionals from literary, healthcare and nature education backgrounds. Some were open events others were for specific client groups.

In the Highlands, people explored their sense of place and learned about the holly tree at Anam Cara, Inverness; they deepened their connection with nature at Moniack Mhor and experienced being at the edge as they explored the breakwater at Lochinver. In Inverness, we led writing sessions with NHS, Mental Health teams and Women's Aid staff and in Abriachan Forest with the Forestry Commission's 'Branching Out' Programme and with Elders with dementia from Glenurquhart Care Home.

In Fife, participants explored seeing with 'owl vision' as they walked on the beach at St Andrews. They set off along the Fife Coastal Path from historic Dysart, walking silently as they wrote from their senses; and wrote as they explored the Mill Burn in the beautiful setting of Falkland Estate. We ran sessions for Year 4 nursing students at Abertay University Dundee, using creative writing to help develop their reflective writing skills.

In Glasgow, we teamed up with VOX-Voices of eXperience and the Glasgow Mental Health Network to work with a group of older people, writing and telling stories as we reflected on where we live, favourite places, and our place in the world.

Everywhere, people wrote and wrote. This anthology brings together just some of the extraordinary writing produced during the project.This project was funded by Awards for All Scotland with support from Glasgow City Council and Scottish Book Trust's Live Literature Fund.

Philippa Johnston
'Writing Place' Project Manager
Lapidus Scotland

'**Write Here**' with Margot Henderson: A creative writing workshop exploring a sense of place and deepening our nature connection.

'**By Holly Leaves We Live**' with Mandy Haggith: Discover some folklore and poetry about holly, and explore the ancient connection between trees, writing, health and happiness.

Here I Am

Here I am
in somebody else's slippers
my toes not quite cosy yet

Here I am
started writing at last
feeling that sigh
as the pen lands on the paper
so do I

Here I am
weaving words
into some kind of pattern
as wibbling as the grain on the wood
but somehow natural, meaningful
essential to my well-being

Here I am
together with you all
entering that quiet
contemplative space

Here I am
Having just found an answer
to the problem
of not having a bell to sound
Hhhmmmm.

Margot Henderson

This Moment

Breathing in the log-warm,
the scented votive
focus inward
and out
life-breath noisy
in the almost silence.

This moment of communion
with my breath,
sustaining me;
heart pumping oxygen molecules about.

This moment
with others
writing out
their own breath

Debbie Ruppenthal

Roominations

Glass sweeps a view
high above
the city,
mountains looming.

Golden drapes
an exit to more
practical concerns.

Hexagonal
view of sky above;
this room
inside,
but out.

Debbie Ruppenthal

Birchskin

Birchskin peels opens its whiteness;
rolls back, reveals an umber lining.
Rosettes of lichen adorn its smooth trunk
- fur on silk.
Mapping its growth with such simple beauty:
would that I age with such grace –
wear scars with pride;
that others may see them as tattoos of life.

Val Fellows

Win-Dow *

Trees in the foreground
telephone masts close behind
even these telephone masts
need trees to exist

Land lies like a bed
sky wrapped in a soft cloud quilt
sun gently rising
slowly waking from night's sleep

A row of stones
an Earth Dragon's vertibrae
rising from the ground.
Is She yawning or roaring?

Prayer flags hanging
on each branch of every tree
Geese string their prayers
in the sky

Margot Henderson

*(Home made form, like haiku. 4 lines: 2 short, 2 long, on looking
out of the window.)

I Am

I am sky
and light
and atmosphere
surrounding
and supporting you
ever changing
constant.

I am a wee thing
You have no name for me
You never notice
and if you do
I threaten death.

I am a wee thing
part of the same chain
of life as you tiny
but not insignificant.

We are nature too,
Walking
absorbing
what you would speak
to our haughty separateness.

Not other or better,
formed from the same
motes of stardust
sharing this giddy planet.

Scrubby gorse lies quiet
waiting to flame the hillside
in yellow glory.
Fellow writers write
absorbed in the hill and sky
Wolves of words captured.

Debbie Ruppenthal

Words for leaves and berries

"Patient Defender"
"Lord of the winter woods"
Defender
Patient guardian
Thorns protecting
Without
Shielding within

Defender
Winter Lord
Prickles speaking
Strength

Defender
Guarding secrets
Soft, round, red
Berries
Protecting
The future.

Ancient Guardian
Of Myth and legend
Standing still
To hedge our boundaries
Brighten our homes
With winter red and green

Bright Thing
In the dark forest
A thorny home
For beast and bird

Bright thing
Jewel of winter
Glossy grace
In darkened places.

We cut your bough
For decoration;
Craftsmen value still
Your strong grain.

Debbie Ruppenthal

Holly

I am the tree of low tide
I do not fail when others fail
I keep my leaves on

male or female
inhabiting extremes
sharp and shiny
glossy and spiny

a poultice of leaves mends broken bones
do not burn me
I am protection

look up
it is safe here
no need for prickles

I stand unfaltering
as light
ebbs

do not fade as others fade
bear witness through the cold time
bear witness to the dark

Mandy Haggith

'Write Here' with Larry Butler: A creative writing workshop exploring a sense of place and deepening our nature connection.

'Nature Notes' with Jayne Wilding: This writing workshop will explore walking as a path to writing for health and wellbeing.

The Scores, St. Andrews

A hall of words enclosed in semi-solid
walls of yellow sandstone hewn
from rocks where pterodactyls roosted
like elegiac dons of English Literature.
Look carefully. There's ripple marks beneath
those chiselings in squared-off blocks.
Because we squirm at nakedness
in gardens, we cover over earth
and fear with imitative tarmac
constellations, tubes of steel

But rosemary remembers, above
the hushing of the Summer plantings,
above the seagulls' constant anguish,
that shocking truth which turned
the sky to everlasting blue.

Lindsay Macgregor

Rocks

Rocks like the backs of beasts.
Walruses ; primordial, green-slimed;
pitted with welts, pock-marked with
spouts and snouts and cup-holes
Deep pockets like the pinch of
fingers in wet clay.

Sandra Ireland

Drooping Daffodils

Hunched low, hidden from the tempest of sight,
seeking sunlight, a moment's warmth:
enough to bask in glory,
if only for a little while.
Yellow festoons the high precipice,
a nodding of gratitude to the coastline,
for providing shelter.

Thank you to the daffodils,
for their vibrant colour and amazing tenacity,
clinging to sides of cliffs, in inhospitable conditions.

A swathe of colour infuses the land,
inviting those at sea to come and celebrate
the warmth and colour of nature.
Seagulls fly overhead, swooping
over the flowers in irreverence,
not needing the soothing beauty as I do.
They seek simple pleasures of food,
fish from the waters,
or discarded morsels from the ground,
left by human hands.

The daffodils do not care, or worry,
but nod in greeting to the wind,
accepting their fate calmly.
They simply exist,
not bound by ego or logic.
They have their moment: shining
and reflecting the joy of Spring.

Craig Gilbert

The Weaving

I've walked the boundary
of my chosen land;
Intrepid expeditions
toward the horizon.

Writing can be hard
when you think too long;
Step outside,
let the openness set you free.

Create a safe space,
write yourself to resolution;
Bring yourself back into this life...
Allow words to be enclosed in ripples.

Caren Gilbert

The Fields

I used to walk along the gravel paths,
and dirt tracks
in the dry fields behind the house,
and grab the heads of grass,
not stopping, just pulling their seeds
into bunches between finger and thumb.
"Cock or hen?" I'd say,
Then I'd scatter them around me,
as I ran on.
Is there time to go back
and see if those seeds have grown?

Louise Liddell

Words for Well-being

Space and place,
found in healing words.
Meet each other,
briefly experience the impact
on our awareness.

Work with the old
to map the new.
Listen deeply,
notice your response.
Spread out
in reflections.
Let your imagination soar
in proportion with the space
above your head.

Don't worry about things making sense,
keep writing until the fear disappears;
There is joy
in witnessing the glee
of writers creating.

Caren Gilbert

Boundary

I've walked to the boundary of my chosen land
As far as I can in time.
The neighbouring land is sea;
Gentle, soothing, swelling power
Recedes graciously,
Hisses occasionally,
Frothing and filling
The crevices of my land
Darkening inches higher each time
Infringing, invading, engulfing,
But there is no forgetting
That my land is yours
Is shaped by you
Slopes into you
And becomes host to your needs.

Louise Liddell

I Come From

I come from a pause,
from a waiting,
and from an uncertain limbo.

I come from silence,
from anger,
and from hiding up the stairs.

I come from invisibility,
from disappointment,
and from the danger of being heard.

I come from compromise,
from negotiation,
and from begging to be allowed to play.

I come from that Summer,
confined to the garden,
without hope of early release.

I come from lies,
from hiding failure,
and from keeping people happy.

I come from isolation,
from self-imposed exile,
and from insanity.

I come from sadness,
from grief,
and from standing in the shadows.

I come from watching others,
drowning in the pain of living,
and from helplessness.

I come from words,
from wounds,
and from healing.

I come from the stars,
from possibilities,
and from adventures.

I come from answers,
from forbidden whys,
from following a path.

I come from strength,
from resilience,
and from survival.

I come from my past,
from my future,
and from dreams to be lived.

Caren Gilbert

Safe places I knew as a child

Sitting on the toilet reading comics
the door locked – Donald Duck, Micky Mouse,
Goofy, Superman, Bugs Bunny, Elmer Fudd
I could sit for hours with a pile of comics

Up a pine tree swaying at the top
looking out across the neighbourhood
I could climb trees all day, slide down branches
and build a tree house with my friend Donny

Swimming in clear lake on hot summer days
underwater weaving through tullies and bulrushes
diving off the pier, water skiing with Bob & Bill
I could swim all day till my skin wrinkled

On grandma & grandpa's postage stamp farm
collecting eggs, digging worms for bait, catching frogs
with bare hands, I could play all day running naked
with my cousin between rows of corn

Swinging on a hammock between willows
dragon flies buzzing over the pond
I could lie here for hours day dreaming
I could lie here all day doing nothing

Larry Butler

Islander

Sea, make a stranger of me.
Erode my familiar features,
make me new
to a landscape that knows
I never belonged.

Shore, make a new friend of me,
not an old acquaintance come to
reconcile.
Forget that I came once
and left with the tide.

Mountains, make me gaze in wonder
as I pass beneath snow capped peaks.
Do not loom
like spectres of the life
I left among you.

Rain, make me run for shelter.
Soak me in an icy downpour,
not in cloud
that formed years ago
and has yet to lift.

Doe, make me an enemy.
Raise a cautious head from grazing
as I pass.
My footstep is changed
and unfamiliar.

Home, make me a welcome guest.
Keep my heart, but I cannot be
yours alone.
I will come often,
a stranger each time.

Louise Liddell

MONIACK MHOR May 2014

'Write Here' with Margot Henderson: A creative writing workshop exploring a sense of place and deepening our nature connection.
Life Writing with Cynthia Rogerson

This Writers' Room

This writers room a mirror
a mirror in the room
these words on paper
mirroring, making room

The mirror on the wall
a church window
that opens to a holy place
offering a greater sense of space
a clear reflection of what is

This room a love spoon
where carved knot-works interlace
a key to the heart's own treasure chest
Old stones nestling against the wind
huddling, remembering
the stories told and shared

This room a shelter from the storm
a refuge from the world
a shawl to wrap around the fragile human form

Margot Henderson

Here I Am

Here I am -
whirling dervish,
mind buzzing,
looking for calm.
Here I am -
in a cosy room
with new faces,
new connections,
new beginnings.
Here I am -
stepping out
in my new guise.
I am a writer!
Here. Now. Today.
Not yesterday's loser
or tomorrow's failure.
Here I am now.
A writer writing
wee words on a new page.
Words of hope, clarity
and charity to myself.

Connie MacDonald

Breathing Space

The smell of fresh toast floated up the narrow winding stairs and under the white cottage door, introducing the awakening dawn. The summer sun peeped through the windowpanes and cast the shadows of dancing trees onto the coombed ceiling. The room was warm; it was warmth of safety and comfort, warmth which would bring someone back to feel held and nurtured. It was a small room, a room which would be remembered forever.

Down stairs the fire cracked and the flames danced, urged on by the seeping resin from newly cut logs. Even though the sun shone and the birds sang, the stone walls of the cottage held onto the evening chill. The fire was welcoming, beckoning her to sit and drink coffee, eat warm buttered toast, and watch the little old lady bustling around the room; she would hold this moment safe in her heart.

Outside the wood pigeons called, as the smell of warm pine and wood smoke indulged the senses. Horses in the paddock stood at the gate, tails swishing away the irritating summer flies, forelocks hanging over their sleepy eyes. Dyke walls bordered the fields, the resilient moss adding flashes of uneven verdant patches.
Lazy clouds drifted over the blue sky as the early heat haze shimmered over the road leading to the village store.

It was the village store, which sold everything, and smelt of soft pink sweeties. Fallen pinecones crunched under foot and she picked them up, and put them into a small wicker basket for the fire to burn.
In the evening they would sit by the fire, the stars would watch them from the black velvet sky, before the wooden shutters were closed. The little caged bird that danced and sang was silenced, as the old man lovingly covered his cage with a small blanket. He must sleep too.

Suddenly a voice spoke and the music stopped. She sat up in the bed as her husband stood, shaking his head. "Here you are," he stated the obvious, smiling, "dreaming again."

"No I wasn't dreaming, I was remembering, I was in my special place. I can't have it back so I go there in my head." She sounded irritated at his interruption. She was just about to go back into the warm room, 'In her head'

"You are terrible for holding onto the past. Playing this music and drifting away." He sat down beside her. In her head she was there, and it was real. She smelt everything, heard everything and held her grandmothers hand. While it was in her heart it was never in the past.

They say "The past is a foreign country, never to be revisited". She would revisit this place whenever she wanted to, savouring every detail that her memory would be generous enough to allow. It was the place from her childhood, with grandparents and love. She missed those days; the days that should have been immortally blessed. In her mind they still could be. There she could escape to a place that as a child she did not recognise as a heaven on earth. This released her from a world of stresses and worries if only for a moment. It was her breathing space.

Rising from the bed she followed her husband out of the door, the scent of warm pine needles still hanging in the air, and she smiled.

EVERYONE SHOULD ALLOW THEMSELVES A LITTLE BREATHING SPACE. RELEASE YOUR MIND IF ONLY FOR FIVE MINUTES EVERY DAY. GO TO YOUR FAVOURITE PLACE AND JUST BE. JUST RELAX, REMEMBER PRACTICE MAKES PERFECT. REWARD YOUR MIND, IT DESERVES IT.

Wendy Simmonds

The Garden

Pinks shivering in the breeze,
saxifrage shaking in the rain,
thyme creeps, waiting
for summer yet to come.

Questions to Ponder at Moniack Mhor

Do foxes wear gloves?
Do fairies wear boots?
Do angels get cold?
Do ghosts get tired?

Lost

Disorientated on the moor,
clouds cover well-kent places.
North is south.
East is west.
Where am I?

Connie MacDonald

'Coming Home to Here' with Margot Henderson: In the year of Homecoming, a chance to use writing as a practice of mindfulness, a way of coming home to ourselves and our sense of place, to the world within us and the world around us.

'Words, Wood and Water' with Mandy Haggith: Join Mandy on a writing walk through the woods to the stunning White Shore beach and discover how you can use the natural environment as creative inspiration.

Here I Am

I can't believe I actually signed up
and then I arrived at a group
with some new people in it
but here I am
and I got through the dreaded question
"How are you?" by answering
"I'm here."
Do any of us know
where the others in this group are?
What's flitting through minds as we sit and breathe?
Where am I?
I'm unsure.
How am I?
I don't know
Who am I?
I'm not even sure of that any more
I do know I'm not who I was
and most likely won't be again.

As much as I loved most of my life
its been shattered by something out of my control
and here I am
among the wreckage
trying to salvage enough pieces
to put the new 'me'
back together

Here I am
watching the rain on the window
mirroring tears to be shed
at some unknown time
Here I am

Susan MacKenzie

This Moment

The rain is hushing on the roof, red shoes, blue floor, rain on the
roof, quietens itself.
The paper is so smooth, the ink so black. Green pen, purple
trousers, red shoes, blue floor.
Faint scent of incence, a thirst for tea, some gentle plate
movements in the kitchen and some cutting, the sound of lunch.
 A breath, one of the deep ones.
The rocks are washed outside. Smashed, but still rock, still three
billion years old. What arrogance we have. How we've trashed the
place.
A robin considers the rubble pile as home. So does the yarrow,
broom, gorse and bramble. It wants to be a forest .

Mandy Haggith

Haiku

Green grapes on a plate
find themselves to be
truly irresistible
Thirteen bicycles
pointing northwards
but never setting off
Woollen yellow coat
hanging patiently
waiting to be picked
Red paint flaking
you look clumsy
on legs rather than water
Balancing on the curb
arms spread eyes closed
how fast can you go
Jump and be caught
scary but exciting
safe and giddy, again!

Jorine van Delft

Something Surprising
The Wren

How can a thing so fragile and so light
(it probably weighs a few ounces)
be also so strong?
It can survive a winter out in the cold
but is protected by no more than feathers.

Romany Garnett

Harbour Haiku

Rainbows of colours
Shocking pink clashing
With orange and red

She wears her sprays of
Droplets like a mantle
Signalling summer's end

Marooned amidst
a sea of tyres the
boat lies exposed

perforated circles of
steel punctuating
the ridged rood

the lion and the
welly pink
and purple curls

Philippa Johnston

Haiku

Dampness in the breath
a dock full of seeds
brown dead, ready to spread

"Hello what are you doing here?"
"I'm writing a bit."
"Oh that's nice, and isn't the rain heavy."

"The bank owns that boat
it has been sitting there for over a year.
Such a shame, somebody ought to do something."

"A swimmer is due tomorrow.
If it is calm enough she will swim
all the way across to Stornoway."

Romany Garnett

Edges.

Looking at the sea the light and ripples are beautiful
and hypnotic – black, blue, white and grey. The sea sloshes
splashes and slaps the seaweed. The waves roll in
making the sea humpbacked again and again.
The ripples criss and cross and swirl on top of each wave.
The sea could almost be some magic elixir of life,
it looks so dark and gloopy like treacle.
I wonder what is underneath, fish perhaps, who knows.
Over there a different pattern emerges
and further away the incessant criss-crossing of ripples is lost
and it becomes a blanket of blue. It is much calmer to look at
as it appears still and serene.
I love being at the water's edge.

Romany Garnett

Lochinver Breakwater

Beneath lapping weed
Almost mammoths stand. Breath held.
We watch and listen

Twisted rusting limbs
stretch through ragged tansy while
sorrel stands aloof

Pretty little boat
anthropomorphising those
bigger smarter craft

Helen M. Sandilands

What's this edge?

It's now and later. It's the end of the line. It's the new page, empty
of words, beckoning.
    There's a slap of water on weeds, weeds on rock, jokes from
distant islands.
        There's a swish in it, like an otter's tail, as she dives
        into the mystery.
Waves fold in, trying to be silent, to keep their secrets, not wake
the dead. Hush, they say. Listen.
    On Cleat, they are throwing up white water, revelling,
dancing, kicking their heels, capering.
        There is work involved in swimming out from here to
        there, but the surface is calm, the sun's out.
Each ripple is a caress. The further we go, the more we will glitter.

Mandy Haggith

Haiku

ladies mantle leaves
holding raindrops
long after the rain stops

gneiss boulders
veined with gleaming minerals
memories of magma

rock doves chase each other
from lamp post to lamp post
only we miss the sea cliffs

if I eat brambles
will I find a haiku
or just get inky fingers?

two swallows and a wren
like the rubble more than I do
we get used to home

one of Robbie's dead machines
and a rusty oil drum
colour co-ordinated

Mandy Haggith

At The Edge

At the edge
rocks are crushed into sand
by the relentless sea

I've been to the edge
of insanity
where tides of life
are battered on the rocky shores
of brutal reality

And yet now – a quietness meets me
with lilting ripples that calm, soothe
the freshness of the sea breeze
caressing my cheek

You and I have been to the edge
but last time I walked away alone
leaving you at sunset to become
one with the sea and sand
at the edge

Susan MacKenzie

Exploring the Mill Burn with poets Jayne Wilding and Caren Gilbert: Join Lapidus Scotland in the beautiful setting of the Falkland Estate in Fife for an enjoyable and stimulating afternoon of walking, writing and exploring the Mill Burn in the company of others interested in words for wellbeing.

On The Walk

Secret bridge, a place to hide,
or cross with child-like glee.
A tranquil place, wind and stream
combine with a floating sound of being.
Underground, the water
disappears into silence –
its own passage unknown to us above.
Then, further upstream,
steps of cascade,
each vibrant but with a sound
all their own.
It does not stop, but yet it moves
with purpose, with its own
soul of life.

Beside, towering beings become
guardians of the burn,
placed strategically around the landscape,
creating little spots of solitude,
nooks and crannies of contemplation.
How lovely it is to sit,
cocooned in such a spot,
letting the earth and water surge
through me in unconfined grandeur.
Familiar yet unfamiliar terrain,
no rules here. No right or wrong.

With rising mischief I close my eyes,
and take steps forward,
arms outstretched.
The place smiles back at me.
but soon I am drawn back
to the water's edge.
I want to move and flow,
like it does.

I want to slow down,
and fit into this land.
Slosh, sploosh, thunk –
these are playful words.
and the water is so clear and pure.

Sunlight pours off the ripples
in jewels of harmony.
Then there is a struggle,
a path riddled with overgrowth
and thorny bristles.
Is the universe testing my might?
or my ability to follow this path?
I step through, and endure.
Oh fresh, giver of life,
come down from the hill
to sustain me.
Sustain me, you have.

Craig Gilbert

One Hundred Steps Along the Burn

100
Thunder-spilling splash in clouds of bubbling froth
the ripple effect with hidden depths of darkness
the mix of light catching glitter
tiny, middle, large and bold – the pebbles of the burn bed
pushed downstream
sandy depths below the fall
shallows show colour but
is there colour in the depths?

200
How many shades of green can there be –
and are they the ones you see?
How many sounds can each bird make, as they gather overhead?
Seeds sway slowly, waiting
for the Breath of Wind
to scatter and sow
Durer time with a pencil
The more you look, the more you see
Disturbing time reveals the creatures' homes
Can disturbing time reveal our inner creature
or creator
or Creator

Elspeth Salter

Haiku

The dandelion clock
Patiently awaits
It's time to fly

Treelings
Alone, but together
Safe in their playpens

The open gate
Says, come and explore
The wood beyond

Finding the path
The helping hand
Stretched out

Let's play says the sapling
Come and join me
I'm over here

Philippa Johnston

Falkland Hill

The trees try to climb
Up the hillside
But are thwarted.
The hills smiles down at his children
They hug his legs.
He shelters them,
Watching over them
With a father's loving eye.

Sounds of the Burn

The higher the fall
The lower the note

The Feather in the Grass

What have you seen little feather
sitting amongst the reeds
by the burn of Falkland?

I've seen you from above
trying to see your way
I sat on the wings of a buzzard
soaring above your life
I've seen your life-stream
taking strange turns
Its torrents
and its placid pools
I chose today...
to let you hold me
and then, to let me go

Elspeth Salter

Two Haiku

Listen to the wren
drab feathers light up as she
chats of ancient ways

Old oak knuckles down
in brown pasture, dwelling on
the chuckle of the burn

The Comfort of Trees

I lean back against the broadness of the tree. Its bark is cheese-grater rough, weathered and chapped like old skin. But there is a softness in the way its spine folds into mine. The tree reaches for me like an outstretched hand, supporting, sheltering. Fingers of wind shake the canopy. Leaves fall like spring rain.

Sandra Ireland

Falkland Estate on a Fine Saturday

Summer just ending
my career at the same stage.
The trees rustle and whisper
The breeze gets up
The whisper becomes more incessant and louder
I can't hear the birds anymore.
The trees are roaring now
like the blood in my ears
The sleep-depriving inner noises
telling me life is not a breeze anymore
It's becoming a whirlwind
Too much to do. Too little time.
Thirty-nine steps bring me to a small waterfall
where the Mill Burn drops gently into a pond
Fashioned generations ago, to give pleasure.
Today the cadent fall still gladdens the heart
bearing as it does, the sound of all waters
from the dribble at the well to the Thunder
Of Niagara and the seven great oceans.
My blood slows with the flow of the waters
Chattering crows circling the treetops
remind me our big noisy family
in the kitchen before bedtime
in childhood, the bustle before bed.

On its descent from the hill, the Mill Burn
encounters many small falls
as full of bubbles and excitement
as a bottle of champagne.

I remember dancing up the long garden
at 3am on my sixtieth birthday
the path lit by dozens of burning tea lights,
a miniature runway.
I was flying that night

not just from the sparkling wine
but from the sheer joy at reaching sixty
Celebrating with my sister, my friends
my amazing soul-mate of a daughter.
We danced and sang as naturally
as the burn cascading over stones.

Men moved the burn downhill
through pasture land
to fill an ornamental pond
to give pleasure to many.
The sound of the burn
chuckling, dashing, rushing
quieting, singing, sparkling
all the way downhill
celebrates a perfect harmony here
between man and nature.

I love being surrounded by the sound of water
especially when the song swells, falls and swells again
as the Mill Burn does on its orchestrated
descent from East Lomond through Falkland Estate.
Its varying tones remind me of Donegal
sitting with my daughter and her Indian friend
on the beach beneath Fanad Head lighthouse,
rainbowed in sun and spume from the Atlantic
showering crushed shell sand like raindrops,
dribbling handfuls of small rounded pebbles,
dropping bigger stones like depth charges
into the whispering waves of the wide ocean
creating an orchestra of sea and shore
our version of Fingal's cave.

East Lomond rises before me as I sit
with my back to an ancient oak
softened by pale green lichen
showing the clean-ness of the air.

The hill presides like a bishop
over the ceremony of burn heading downhill
to form its union with the sea.
The tall trees stand like ushers
and the wind chants its song.
Sometimes the burn runs underground
through little darkling tunnels
under grassy banks that allow us over
the descent into darkness noisy
but the exit quieter, calmer, chuckling
over stones, glad to be in the open where,
yellow flowers nod and cheer.

Gabriel McNeil

Haiku

A fine day, trees whispering
Water chuckles over stones
It is enough.

Water silent on flat stones
Cascades loudly over falls
Spray and joy.

Birds skimming the pond
Flitting soundlessly on the evening breeze
Tranquility.

Gabriel McNeil

Where Am I?

I am apart
I am rushing along
in the whirling stream,
plunging over the edge.

I am listening
to the unsaid things
hovering overhead,
a gathering of intent.

The wind speaks.
I do not hear.
The wind roars.
I do not hear.

Until, at last, a leaf percussion
raises my head.
I wonder at their song;
the sun dances
in the Mill Burn.

Why Am I here?

I am here
to illuminate,
to sound an alarm
for the rushing
of time.

I am here to welcome,
to open a door
for the unexpected
of happening.
I am here to serve,
to be a comfort
for the falling of being.

Caren Gilbert

GLASGOW October 2014
VOX Seniors Group

Moving Minds
A series of Creative Writing Workshops with **Lesley O'Brien** exploring how our sense of place affects our wellbeing. We'll be writing and telling stories as we reflect on where we live and how we use it, favourite places, and our place in the world.

Glasgow

*G*allus Glasgow opporchancities
*L*ovely lively green parks
*A*mazing architecture
*S*tatues and songs
*G*lasgow tenements
*O*h, I just love it! Oh where is the Glasgow I used to know?
*W*ashhouses, wishes and wally closes.

Oh Where is the Glasgow I used to Know?

Oh where is the Glasgow I used to know?
Outside of a tram, through Parkhead Cross

Oh where is the Glasgow I used to know?
Lex MacLean Show, in The Pavilion

Oh where is the Glasgow I used to know?
Rag and Bone man's, horse and cart

Oh where is the Glasgow I used to know?
Clothes, woollens for a couple of balloons

Oh where is the Glasgow I used to know?
Jingle of the gigs and Rag man's horn

Oh where is the Glasgow I used to know?
Selling brickettes, along The Parade

Oh were is the Glasgow I used to know?
Inside toilet, upstairs to the throne

Oh where is the Glasgow I used to know?

Group Poems

58

Tenement Tale

Solid and sooty black tenement walls surrounded me since birth. Born in the kitchen recess with a gurgle and a cry. Sleeping three to a bed in the bedroom with my brothers. Home was warm and comforting.The kitchen coal fire sparked and the flames danced towards your fingers. The fire grill protected me from burns as I was told. Toasting marshmallows on the fire, waiting for them to cool on a stick. Sweet and warm, they were a treat.

Up until I was three, I thought all houses were black till I saw red and grey sandstone and granite buildings on my travels on the city trams. The bell would be rung by the conductor and off we would shuffle along the tramlines. A three-penny ticket for me and an adult fare for mum – off we would go to the bright lights of the Glasgow City Centre shops.

The shop displays were bright and dazzling; everything to furnish a house and clothes for all. The toys and comics were never ending, The Bimbo, The Dandy and The Beano too. Stories and drawings were a delight to me. Tea and scones with jam and butter at the Charles Rennie Mackintosh Tea Rooms was just the business and ever so polite.

The days were grand. I was wee with red curly hair and a small pot belly, A miniature "Charlie Drake" my parents cried with a laugh. Life was good and sweets were abundant, penny dainties, blackjacks, sour plums, sherbet dabs and aniseed balls too. Sweet dreams were made of this.

Those solid tenement walls would be there I thought would be there till my dying day, demolished in the sixties and red brick terraced houses took their place. No blue plaque for me, I'm not famous you see. However those memories of my childhood are more precious to me than all that fame can bring.

Gordon Fraser

I Feel

I feel like a prisoner when the dark lurgy descends on me. Lying
on the couch not moving, seeing but not watching the TV screen
that sits flickering in a corner of an ever shrinking room.
Is it night or day? Is it Monday or Thursday?
Who knows? Who Cares?

"You're a fucking worthless poor excuse for a man" a voice in my
head tells me. " No job. No money. No wife. No contact with your
daughters. Even the fucking Scouts threw your worthless body
out.
Why bother? Just lie here, go to sleep and never wake up. No one
will know or miss you."

Nine stories up.
A quick hop over the veranda.
Falling.
Falling.
Falling.
Then pain
Followed by...

Donald Hosie

I Feel Free

I feel free when I am on horseback. The feeling of exhilaration when you are galloping through woodland is one of the best, you and the horse in harmony acting as one. The horse trusts you to know where you are going and you trust the animal to follow your instructions without any fear.

The sight of the trees rushing past inches from your face, the smell of the pines and flowers filling your nose, the sunlight on your back as you burst through the shadows into an open glade all make you feel that it is good to be alive.

Suddenly a fallen tree lies across the path and you and your horse take off in a jump, feeling as if you are floating, suspended between land and sky you hang for a heartbeat. Only the sound of the birds and your won heart thumping fills your ears. Then in one flowing motion you hit the ground breaking into the wild rush once again.

God is in his heaven and all is right with the world.

Donald Hosie

Senses

I hear the boisterous infectious laughter of the playful children
I taste the salty out of doors tangy fish and chips from newspaper
I see dangerous, boisterous wild waves
I touch slippery, dry, glittering, flowing soft sand
I smell salty, smothering seaweed?

Jim Owens

I smell freedom
I touch the stars
I hear the screech of the seagulls
I feel hopeful
I see infinity

George Brown

I Like

I like a girl that likes rabbits
I like carrot cake, rich and succulent
I like cinnamon, spicy and sweet
I like cabbage, pungent, thick and irony
I like carpet, Ulster weave
I like broccoli, little green trees
I like brussell sprouts and they like me
but I **really** like a girl that likes rabbits.

Group Poem

From My Window I Can See

From my window I can see
wee Cumbrae's lighthouse beam shining on me.

From My tent I can see
Guides and Brownies having their tea.

From my window I can see
journeying steamers on the squally waves.

From my tent I can see
rain, wind and dance of flowers.

From my window I can see
children playing happily in the sea.

Group Poem

From my window I can see

The to and from of the steamers
on the rise and fall of the sea waves.

The fluffy white clouds perambulating
the bright blue sunlit sky.

The journeying steamers on the squally waves
cotton wool clouds against blue clear sky.

Jim Owens

I Am

I am the moonlight dancing on the white horses
pushing towards the shore

I am the cleansing sea air filling my lungs
I am the relentless waves
crashing on the rocks rythmically

I am serenity on the deserted beach at night
and feel one again with the elements

I am pulsing like fish in the rock pools waiting
for the ocean to return on the tide of time

Gordon Fraser

I Am

I am spring's first sigh - fragile indomitable hope.
I am spring blowing through the soul.
I am singing like the wind, dancing melody.
I am indifferent to soft sweet temptation.
I am Maxie, living, loved forever.

Amanda Wright

Not Your Time

I lick my lips
I taste the sea
and I feel
the morning breeze
in my hair.

I lay on the sand
and feel your hand
please me everywhere.

But it's not your time to stay

The sound of the sea
next to me
as you hold
my heart in
your hand.

The sun it shines
dapples, entwines
apple trees
sweet memories.

But it's not your time to stay

You wipe my tears
and I feel the fear
suffocate my heart.
You hand me sugar
cane rum, limes and ice.

And I know that our time has come

Lesley O'Brien

DYSART October 2014

Writing from the Senses: Join writers Jayne Wilding and Craig Gilbert on a writing walk from Dysart along the Fife Coastal Path exploring the power of writing from the senses and how it contributes to our wellbeing.

Dysart Haibun

I give them strict instructions not to talk when we go outside to walk and write. They concentrate, notice the details and begin to take notes almost as soon as we amble along the streets of Dysart. We stop at a place where we can look out over the sea, only I can't.

> Forgot my glasses!
> the sea
> is a blur

I begin facilitating a writing workshop using the senses to inspire words for health and wellbeing without being able to see properly. I will have to focus on things close up, not distant horizons. We walk into the sunlight and down the Hie-Gait past a house built in 1750 or at least this is what my notebook tells me. I am now scribbling too, stopping to peer at the cobbles and rusty boot-scrapers of old Dysart. The wind is strong and I can smell the sea and hear the noise of the crane down at the harbour. This is the day they take the boats out of the water for winter.

> Last of the boats,
> masts wobble
> in the wind.

At the harbour I notice the pigeons nesting in the walls and scribble a note to myself about them in my green notebook in pencil. I write the name of a boat that's already been lifted to the safety of the quay, 'Valkyrie'.
'Are you from the Courier?' asks a man wearing a peaked cap. He points to my pencil and notebook. I hesitate before I speak, fully aware that I had asked the group not to talk when we went out.

> Do as I
> say
> not as I do!

'We are doing a writing workshop,' I say succinctly, trying to keep the conversation short. But the man in the peaked cap is not deterred.

Sound of wellies
scuffing
the cobbles.

'This,' he says, slapping the belly of the Valkyrie,
'is one of the last of the Dysart yawls!'
'Nice looking boat,' I say courteously.
'She has a dipping lug sail and she was built by a miner.'
That's it! I'm caught like a fish on a hook, caught by a story.
'Can I write that down?'
'On you go,' he says smiling to himself.
So, I write 'dipping lug sail' in big pencil in a small notebook. But
he's going too fast for me to write much... telling me that the
miners built the yawls in their spare time and that they used to
race them out on the Firth of Forth. I'm trying to keep up with
him.
'They carried bags of sand as ballast and sometimes they would
chuck the ballast overboard so they could go even faster.'

*I am now at sea. I am out on the Firth of Forth on a Dysart yawl
chucking a bag of sand over board on a bright windy day like today.
We are neck and neck with another yawl and we want to win the
race.*
'We've still got two bags of sand on board,' I shout.
My crew mate looks shifty and says'
'Chuck it in their boat, that'll slow them down!'
So I do.

A dog barks -
I come back
to my senses.

'Then there were fisticuffs on the pier,' says the man in the
peaked cap.
And I manage to write the word fisticuffs in the notebook before I
thank him for his story and quietly re-join the group.

Jayne Wilding

Exploration of Senses

Stepping into the 7am flat calm,
where all doors are different
and the lines that we are
become visible
in waves on the horizon.

The village green, deserted,
awaiting conversation,
company and warmth.
Weave the autumn leaves
and seagull cries
with the salty sunshine breeze.

Run fingers over silver birch bark,
stripped bare.
Take curiosity and senses to the edge,
Then, take one more step
and stand in cormorant formation.

Wonder at no-longer doorways
leading to impossible destinations.
Breathe deeply the surging waves,
the camaraderie of earth bound gravity.

Steal whispered moments of connection,
allow footsteps to be heard.

Caren Gilbert

Small Acts of Rebellion

Express joy to those who
will listen and to those who will not,
Walk on the edge of silence,
be lifted by stretching shadows.
Be mesmerised by the see-quest
Stand boldly on the prow
of a circular Trojan.

Listen to the slat- grey sea and tunnel-roar,
singing sand-tide stories of yesterday.
Then walk into the wind-whipped woods
to learn 100-year legends from creaking boughs.

Set out, with no sense of time,
taste freedom in every pace,
there is texture in fragments of wild conversation,
watchful eyes surveying every move.

The painted-over rust betrays
the passing of moments,
just as raindrops usher us on.
The jackdaws' melancholic clacks,
children trapped indoors,
time is ever the enemy.

Caren Gilbert

Downhill in Dysart

– An ode to John McDougall Stuart (explorer)

I glimpse Down Under amidst the shards
and dream
I give way past the Tree of Light
whilst Satellite dish bins flock by the clock
5.30 mill rush inscribed in walkers' memory
Did they lift their eyes to the seas?
To the Antipodes?
Like you?

Blinded by sight

Sheershine blinding sea
seen through half-closed eyes
Ghost of a boat
in and Out
of Blinked clarity

Elspeth Salter

Untitled

Coloured art glinting in the sun
opens up the journey to the sea,
Clouds whizzing by with increasing wind,
a beauty to stand and gaze upward at the big sky.
Unknown words etched in stone,
overlooked by many,
a wonder at times gone by.
The sea shimmers in steady motion,
flowing with eternal majesty,
as I stand and stare at its expanse.

Six birds sit on a lone rock,
just waiting, or watching, at the swirl of waves.
Intricate white buildings nestle in romantic notions,
with the slopes leading to the sea.
The wind threatens and billows
among the tiny lanes, a physical presence felt –
the sea is king here.
White froth spills over rocks as clouds obscure
the warmth on the way to the harbour.
Distant islands and land leave the mist on the horizon,
showing off their crags.

Not a soul can be seen from the houses,
poised for the oncoming storm –
and I pause, observing the quiet streets,
yet feeling so wonderfully alive,
as organic and mutable as the crashing waters.
Further, there is movement in the harbour –
where boats are lifted by a noisy mechanic crane
to escape the storm to come.

Boats are bobbing up and down,
and land is lost to mist.
Fishermen gather and talk in low voices.
Dogs bark their cries of dissent,
as people's footsteps hurry over cobbles.
Under cave, sound is muffled, but echoes channel through
to a sandy shore, the feel of the sand a comfort to the gusts
surrounding me.

Craig Gilbert

An Appropriate Scale

Man's mark is small but without it I have no scale
in the midst of windwild water and tide
Hints on the horizon
Chimneys
One Bright Light.
Close by, the manmade builtscape
tries to offer shelter.
The crane lifts small boats to safety.
Strange blue pillars
cannot reach the simple elegance
of one gull gliding

Signs of the Times

Can signs lead me?
"Caution Unstable Ground"
"Reduce Speed Now"
"Path Closed"
Which way will the next wave take me?
Pulling me back or carrying me?
or with the glide of the gull soaring on the currents of the air?
Will a crane be there to lift me from once safe harbours,
now threatened by storm?
Will Man or Nature lead me?
Both have weathered me
and time will wear me down
as the sandstone worn to sand beneath
my feet
and the piece in my pocket
to remind me
when present facts are
gone.

Elspeth Salter

74

ABRIACHAN Forest October 2014

Words in the Woods with Branching Out.
and **What's The Story** with Glenurquhart Centre.
Margot Henderson

Forest Haiku

Sunlight on pine branches
browning birch leaves on the path
gold grasses waving as we go by

Voices echoing up ahead
the squelch of footsteps in puddles
the rustle of a page turning

Sun on my back
toes tingling in my boots
air in my nostrils

A wee straggle of us on the path
the odd blether of voices
followed by a laugh

Margot

This Moment

Translucent smoke in sunlight
the sound of silence rejuvenating
peacefulness
voices carried on the wind
dark, light, translucent grey
indescribable shades of green

Nathalie

This Moment

A silky web glistening in the sun
golden grass low and high
browning pines gently moving
in the breeze
the blue sky
looking down

the sound of something man made
disrupting the peace
of the trees

the crackle and ping of the fire
engulfing, burning,
simmering the wood

the beautiful song
of a feathered friend
high up in the trees

the chill of the bark
beneath my base
unlike a tree
un-natural to me

Bethany

Branching Out

Branching out just like a tree
here's how the forest is growing me
there's something comforting
being out in the depth of nature
brings your mind to peace
at peace with the forest

Bethany

Branching out is growing me
I am nature
nature is me
branching out is part of me

Nathalie

The moss is rising up the tree
from the ground.
The bracken is glowing in the sunshine.
The sun is shining on the trees.
The cones are falling from the trees.

Branching out is growing me in the woods.
Its good to get out and feel
the freedom of the woods.

Callum

Tree Song

Just like the tree
I shall be free
living my life
as I want to be
Sunshine in my heart

Anne Marie

This Forest Is

Tranquility
Its so quiet
No traffic noise
None of the usual humdrum

Walking through the hills and trees
the peace

I look forward to it
It's a break
from the usual routine

You are on your feet and moving about.

Kevin

This Forest Is

Freedom to do what you like
The people are friendly
It's a change of scenery
You don't feel the benefits till after.

It gets me moving
It gets me active
It's a place of beauty

You know its always been like that
ever since the Bronze Age
you just wonder what they got up to.

It gives me an enjoyable glow
a sense of freedom.
The trees give me a sense of time
1000's of years.

A cup of tea tastes better in the woods
The fire gives me a warm glow
peacefulness and a calm head

You go back feeling more relaxed
more at peace with yourself
tired too, which is good

It is enjoy-full doing the fire
and seeing it lit

Grace

I like getting out for a walk
It takes your mind off other things
Its different being outdoors
It's a nice change
a safe environment
You feel freer here

David

Winter's coming
shadows getting longer
birds getting quieter
trees getting barer
wind getting colder
bracken getting browner

Roll on Spring

Its easier to relax
outside than inside
in the woods
there's no pressure

Dominic

This Forest Is

The shade between the tall fir trees
quiet and dark
the dead of grey,
misty dampness on the ferns.
the bark of the trees
like ancient dead crocodiles
everything quiet, silent.

The trees reaching up towards
the blue of heaven
quiet, peace.
A solitary bird tweets
beneath a droning aeroplane.
A few branches silently shiver
in the cold chilly air
my nose cold,
my cheeks icy
my feet snug in my boots

I'm branching out just like a tree
here's how the forest is growing me
makes my legs dangle
healthy and alive
Oh joy! Give me five!

Group Piece

My Cathedral

I live in the woods every day.
God made my Cathedral for me.
Jim Reeves said it.
That's why I don't go to church.
I don't need to.
The carpet that I kneel on
was made by His right hand

I love Abriachan
the peace and quiet
the beauty and the sincerity
of both the people
and the forest
the changing of the seasons.

I grew up on the Isle of Skye
I had a lighthouse for a neighbour.
I used to sit at my bedroom window
watching the lighthouse
light up the cliff.

I am at home in the forest.
Give me a wide open space
any day of the week.
I am glad I am back in the hills.

Christine

What's the Story
Glenurquhart Elders Group

Here in the forest it is beautiful
Lovely weather
Relaxing, peaceful

We didn't hear any birds did we?

Do we get birds in these trees here?
chaffinches, sparrows, blackbirds,
blue-tits, robins, thrush.

We were looking for fish in the pond
but we didn't see any.

A thatched hut down there
What's that for?

That's for doing your business
That's Taigh Beag
The Wee House

Glenurqhart Elders Group

Trees

Trees are beautiful
when you see their shape.

Not so much the conifers
more the other ones.

They are just as beautiful as flowers

I like a tree
the shapes, the clefts in the bark
the big roots

The old trees are huge

I always think
of what they could tell you
if they could talk

On the Isles
there are no trees.
no Autumn

I love trees
but if you have a lovely view
you might not see it

Near me there are trees planted in the 1960's
They are all grown now
and they cut off my view of the Black Isle

The Places We Love Best
(Talking round the table with a cup of tea)

I would go out on the hills
in my walking days
Now we are in our staggering days

In Belladrum
Phoineas Hill
is the highest hill
You could see 4 counties from there
on a nice day

If the trees were cut
You could see the loch from my window
Rhychraggon

Glasgow is
Friendly people
High buildings
They weren't so high once
That's where I was born
3 stories and no lift

I was 4 weeks old when we came to Beauly
The whole family came to be safe during the war
We walked 4 miles with our cases

Home is a safe place
where everything is familiar
and its nice and warm
an open fire and a hot bath

My flat in Beauly is very quiet,
up the back of Beauly
Near the Kessock Bridge, Queen Mary's Road.
The view is lovely over the loch
and the whole village
You feel like you are miles away.
When my son comes home
it is the first place
where you would get a good view over Loch Ness

I love Glen Affric
The views, the walks
Miles from anywhere
The beauty of majestic hills
The memories

Amanda, Avis, Eileen, Elizabeth, Jackie, Jessie, Jim, John, John, Margaret

Acknowledgements

'Writing Place' has been very much about partnership and collaboration and we would like to thank the many individuals and organisations who have offered help and support. While many of the workshops and events were open to all, we also worked with the following groups and organisations:

Highlands
Cairdeas Cottage, Inverness;
NHS Highland: Support In Mind Scotland
Suzanne Barr at Abriachan Forest Trust
the Branching Out Programme, Forestry Commission Scotland;
Christine Mathieson Glenurquhart Library
Care Staff at the Glenurquhart Centre
Margaret Kearney at Anam Cara;
Sharon Bartram at Assynt Leisure Centre, Lochinver;
Keith Walker at Highland Council;
Graham Morgan at HUG (Highlands Users Group);
Imran Arain at NHS Highlands
Terry Page, Ross-shireWomen's Aid
Rachel Humphries and Cynthia Rogerson at Moniack Mhor - Scotland's Creative Writing Centre;
Margot Henderson (Regional Co-ordinator, Highlands);

Fife
Chris Jones at the University of St Andrews School of English; Year 4 Honours Degree Nursing Students undertaking the Adult and Mental Health Community Pathway
Dawn Coleman at Abertay University Dundee;
Tanya Duthie at Dundee Central Library;
Ninian Stuart at Falkland Centre for Stewardship;
Shona McEwan at Fife Council;
Yvonne Melville at Fife Cultural Trust Libraries Service;
Fife writers, Caren Gilbert and Craig Gilbert;
Jayne Wilding (Regional Co-ordinator Fife)

Glasgow
Mahmud Al-Gailani atVOX-Voices of eXperience
Glasgow Mental Health Network
Glasgow Women's Aid.
Live Active, Glasgow Life / Glasgow Sport;
Maggie's
Gartnavel General Hospital
Ann Wales and Christine Cather at NES Scotland
Larry Butler and Lesley O'Brien
(Regional Co-ordinators Glasgow)

and

Mel Parks, Christine Hollywood and Vicky Field at Lapidus UK;
Daniel Abercrombie
Donald Smith at the Scottish Storytelling Centre;
Gail Aldam and all at SMHAFF

We would like to thank the following writers and storytellers who
have led workshops and given readings, making 'Writing Place' such
a success:

Ted Bowman;
Larry Butler
Allison Galbraith
Valerie Gillies;
Mandy Haggith
Margot Henderson
Alexander Hutchison
Paula Jennings
Ruth Kirkpatrick;
Gerry Loose
Lindsay Macgregor
Aonghas MacNeacail
Lesley O'Brien

Cynthia Rogerson
Maureen Sangster;
Jayne Wilding

Philippa Johnston for Co-ordinating the Project
The Management Committee of LAPIDUS Scotland,
For the Right Reasons

We are grateful for the generous financial and in-kind support we have received for this project from: Awards for All Scotland; Glasgow City Council; Scottish Book Trust's Live Literature Fund; Fife Cultural Trust; Dundee Libraries; and The Royal Society of Edinburgh Young Academy of Scotland.